What They A

"The *Day Break* me............., and reflective, and they represent an astute, spiritual perspective."
                              Linda Nease Scott, M.Ed., Ed.D.

"*Day Break* is a dose of inspiration for the heart and mind."
                              Gary Morsch, M.D., M.P.H.
                              Founder of Heart to Heart International;
                              Author, The Power of Serving Others

"I highly recommend *Day Break* to those who seek inspiration and challenge."
                              Loren Gresham, M.A., Ph.D. –
                              President Emeritus, SNU

"*Day Break* provides timeless inspiration and encouragement to start your day."
                              Sylvia Goodman, M.A., Ed.D., ATC

"*Day Break* gives us a treasure of Dr. Barnard's fresh and spiritually-uplifting encouragement."
                              Robert L. Parker, Former Senior Corporate Officer,
                              Beverly Enterprises

"Tom Barnard is a trusted guide for any who hear the daily call to follow Jesus."
                              Grayson L. Lucky, M.A., Th.M., D.D.,
                              Affiliate Faculty, Phillips Theological Seminary

==

Additional Comments Are Available on Page 124

==

Day Break

Thomas Elliott Barnard, M.A., Ed.D.

Copyright © 2018

All rights reserved.
No part of this book may be reproduced or transmitted in any form or by any means, electronic or mechanical, including photocopying, recording or by any information storage and retrieval system, without written permission from the author.

Day Break

Start Your Day With

Magnificent Thoughts

Thomas Elliott Barnard, M.A., Ed.D.

Introduction

Have you ever read a book that was written in such a way that you could open it to any page and begin reading without skipping a beat with what was inside? Have you ever thought how nice it would be to begin at the end of a book and read forward to the beginning?

Day Break is the book for you! Fact is, you don't even have to search the *Table of Contents* to find a topic that interests you. There is no table of contents in this book! If you are really curious about what's inside, go to the very end of the book for an index listing of the titles that make up the contents. Better yet—open the book to any page and begin reading. Follow your heart from there.

Day Break is a collection of short meditations for serious Christians of all ages and educational levels. A kid of 17 and a senior adult of 97 will find the contents understandable and relevant to their walk with God. You will find humor as well as pathos, but neither will lead to depression on your part. There are stories as well as anecdotes. There are Scriptures as well as memorable quotes. Each meditation ends with a brief, personal prayer.

Day Break began years ago as a weekly meditation that enjoyed a large following over the Internet. The original title was "Friday Evening", and subscriptions grew very quickly— at one time over two thousand readers in 35 world areas were on the email list. A friend entered Friday Evenings on his personal website, making them readily available to anyone with a computer anywhere in the world.

Day Break contains the best-of-the-best essays from "Friday Evenings." The meditations are non-sectarian and theologically mainstream. Although the readers of Friday Evenings come from a variety of theological persuasions, we received very few complaints about the theological positions of the several writers who contributed to the publication.

Welcome to *Day Break*. Our prayer is that those who read these pages will be drawn closer to God and to the eternal truths contained in Scripture.

Thomas Elliott Barnard – M.A., Ed.D.

Ask and Keep Asking

Have you ever wondered if God answers prayers from everyone? Or just from good people?

George lived in a modest house adjacent to the church. The pastor heard he was ill and decided to visit George and assure him that the church would be praying for him. The front door of George's house was open, and only a screen door kept folks and animals from walking right in. The pastor called to him from the porch, and George said, "Come in." He was lying on his bed near the rear of the house. After a short conversation, the pastor asked him if he could pray for the man. George was blunt. "It won't matter none. God only hears one prayer: 'God, be merciful to me, a sinner.'" Was George right?

He was half right. Does God hear the prayers of penitent sinners? Of course. God hears prayers. Period. He listens. The fact that your hopes are unmet is not due to God's insensitivity. Often it is because you have not asked.

Ask, and keep on asking until you receive an answer from God. That's the way it works.

> "If you then, being evil, know how to give good gifts
> to your children, how much more
> will your Father who is in heaven
> give good things to those who ask him."
> (Matthew 7:11 NKJV)

> "My horse was very lame,
> and my head did ache exceedingly.
> Now what occurred I here avow is truth
> let each man account for it as he will.
> Suddenly I thought,
> 'Cannot God heal man or beast as He will?'
> Immediately my weariness
> and headache passed;
> and my horse was no longer lame."
> John Wesley's Journal

Heavenly Father, I know I have missed untold blessings and answers to prayer because I assumed you were too busy to listen. So I didn't ask; I didn't want to bother you with a minor problem. I am sure I have prayed at times—in ignorance—for things that were selfishly motivated. Wesley's experience has reminded me that you are very much interested in what interests me, and if I would just seek your will, half the battles of my life could be won. Remind me of this truth each time I am reluctant to share with you the things that bug me every day of my life. Amen.

Be Happy—It Beats Worry Every Time

Early in the history of flight a pilot ventured to fly solo around the world. His plan called for him to schedule a place to land about every four hours, adding fuel as necessary. After his first scheduled refueling stop, he was about half way to his next destination when he heard a strange gnawing sound in his aircraft, like something alive chewing on something metallic. Rats were known to do such things. Fear struck the pilot. Could it be that a rodent was gnawing on a vital cable inside his plane? What should he do?

The pilot remembered that rodents cannot survive in high altitudes. So he pulled back on the controls, guiding the plane in an upward trajectory. Eventually the gnawing sound stopped. When the plane landed safely about two hours later, a dead rat was found on board. The pilot and his plane were safe.

In our spiritual journey, sometimes we are visited by unwelcome guests—worry, stress, even old age. What can we do? Clovis Chappell offers a simple solution: "Worry dies when we ascend to the Lord through prayer and His Word." Happiness in the soul begins there. Try it—you may like it.

> "Therefore I say to you, do not worry about your life,
> what you will eat; nor about the body,
> what you will put on. Life is more than food,
> and the body is more than clothing."
> (Luke 12:22-23)

> "Here's a little song I wrote
> You might want to sing it note for note
> Don't worry, be happy
> In every life we have some trouble
> But when you worry you make it double
> Don't worry, be happy
> Don't worry, be happy now."
> Robert McFerrin, Jr.

Heavenly Father, I confess that worry finds me when I least expect it. It often occurs in the dark of night, when I am alone. I try to deny that it exists, but it is there, reminding me that I can't overcome it on my own. When worry strikes, teach me to find that secret place in prayer. Remind me that you have invited me to bring all of my concerns to you, including my fears and anxieties. I know that worry is a destructive force. Teach me to trust you more and worry less. In the strong Name of Jesus I pray. Amen.

Cherish the Good Times Forget the Bad

Ask any bright, twelve-year-old girl about the source of the name, "Ebenezer," and she will probably say, "Scrooge's first name." She would be correct, of course. The old guy with a twisted nose and fractured spirit was memorialized in Charles Dickens' story, *Christmas Carol*.

Actually, the first Ebenezer was a stone—not a person. After years of spiritual backsliding, military debacles, and moral failure, Israel repented under the leadership of Samuel—Israel's first judge. In memory of this major national turnaround, Samuel selected a large stone (actually, a boulder) and placed it between the towns of Mizpah and Shen in Israel as a monument to God's help and faithfulness. First Samuel 7:12 reads:

"Samuel took a stone and set it between Mizpah and Shen, and named it Ebenezer, saying, 'Thus far the Lord has helped us.'"

The Ebenezer Stone represented a new beginning—a marker-event in the history of God's people.

Do you have some memories from your past that haunt you? You may still remember—in full color and hi-definition—the bad times in your life, and fail to remember the good times. God wants you to turn that around—celebrate the victories and forget the failures. He will help you. Ask him.

> "Forgetting the past and looking forward
> to what lies ahead, I strain to reach
> the end of the raceand receive the prize
> for which God, through Christ Jesus,
> is calling us up to heaven."
> (Philippians 3:13-14 NLT)

> "Here I raise my Ebenezer;
> hitherto by Thy help I've come,
> And I hope by Thy good pleasure
> safely to arrive at home."
> Robert Robinson - Lyrics:
> "Come Thou Fount of Every Blessing"

Heavenly Father, when I reflect on my own Ebenezer stones of the past, I am encouraged to face my trials today with renewed vigor and faith. Help me build some new Ebenezer stones to remind me of the victories you have allowed me to enjoy. Help eradicate from my memory the sins of the past (that you have already forgiven and forgotten), and help me remember the fresh victories of days past. Amen.

Defeat Temptation--Look to Jesus

Have you ever wondered why famous people say some of the dumbest things? Particularly writers, actors, and politicians. Occasionally yours truly! But not today. It's time to get serious. You're on the right page. Proceed.

In *The Picture of Dorian Gray*, author Oscar Wilde wrote, "The only way to get rid of temptation is to yield to it." Right! That might work in theater, but not in real life. And especially not in the life of the Christian!

For the believer, temptation should not be ignored, justified, or facilitated. Jesus was a real human being. More than once he faced the Tempter. And Jesus not only resisted him—he overcame him! Destroyed his arguments. Jesus wants to help you do the same.

Do you remember what Jesus did to overcome temptation during his forty days in the wilderness? He quoted the Word of God! Check it out: Matthew, Chapter 4:1-11. So, how should *you* answer Satan when you are tempted? With Scripture! It works. And the Spirit of Jesus will also help you when you face temptation.

> "Because he (Christ) himself suffered
> when he was tempted,
> he is able to help those who are
> being tempted."
> (Hebrews 2:18 NIV)

> "A current silly idea is that good people
> do not know what temptation means.
> This is an obvious lie. Only those
> who try to resist temptation
> know how strong it is.
> A man who gives in to temptation
> after five minutes simply does not know
> what it would have been like an hour later.
> That is why bad people in one sense
> know very little about badness.
> They have lived a sheltered
> life by always giving in."
> C.S. Lewis – Mere Christianity

Lord, as a young Christian, it never occurred to me that you—the Son of God—were exactly the right person to come to my aid during my temptations. You were tempted when you lived on earth, and you were victorious. I have since learned that Satan wants me to believe that when I experience temptation, I am at fault—and I am alone! It is comforting to realize that you walked these roads before me and understand what I am facing even before temptations arrive. Thank you for helping me understand this powerful truth. Amen.

Do One Thing Very Well

Have you ever stayed at a hotel where everything you experienced was exceptional—from the moment you checked in until the moment you checked out? This is a story about one such visit.

John was a frequent traveler to cities in the east. On one of his trips he stayed at a hotel in Frederick, Maryland. In many ways the stay was like other hotel stays. But there was something different about this one. At the registration desk John was impressed by the cheerfulness of the person at the reception desk. When he commented on it, she replied, "We have the friendliest Inn anywhere in the country." Big claim, John thought. But when he arrived at his room and began unpacking, he noticed a printed card on the table by the phone. The note began with the standard marketing word, "Welcome." What followed next was far from standard.

> "All of us here have only one job to do…
> to provide you with the
> best hotel accommodations,
> service, and value available today."

The employees of that hotel understood that above everything else in their job description, they had "one

job to do." It was more than a cliché. It meant quality of service, cleanliness, customer satisfaction, room comfort level, amenities, and anything else that one could list. It was a powerful mission statement reduced to just four words—"one job to do."

The Apostle Paul might have had something like that in mind when he wrote to the Church at Corinth. His expectations were high; time and resources were short. So he focused on the singularity of his purpose. Paul had one job to do—not forty things to dabble in. Will you strive to follow his example?

> **"Do you not know that in a race
> all the runners compete,
> but only one receives the prize?
> So run that you may obtain it. Every athlete
> exercises self-control in all things. They do it
> to receive a perishable wreath,
> but we are imperishable."**
> (1 Corinthians 9:24-25 RSV)

> **"Well done is better than well said."**
> Benjamin Franklin

Heavenly Father, continue to reveal to me what the important aspects of the Christian life are. Give me the wisdom to separate the most important from the less important. Then help me prioritize things so that the single most important priorities in my life rise above all other priorities. In the strong name of Jesus I pray. Amen.

Face Your Challenges...Courageously

Do you enjoy Bible stories? Here's one—The army of Israel desperately needed a champion. Saul—Israel's king—was definitely not the man. Israel had an army, but most of them were common men—farmers, shepherds, husbands, dads. They had numbers, but not enough to go against the Philistines.

Israel's enemy had a champion—Goliath—a monster of a man who was a foot taller than any of the Israelite soldiers. And he possessed weapons of war—a spear, a shield, and a massive sword. Against a champion like this, no Israelite had a chance. Until boy-David showed up. All he had were the "weapons" of a sheepherder: a hand-made sling and a handful of smooth stones from a stream.

Young David was naïve, but he was also very brave. He didn't see the army of the Philistines; he saw one man. He didn't take on the entire army; he took on one man, albeit a giant man. Had David looked more objectively at the situation, he might have taken flight back home to his father. But he didn't! He stayed. And he won.

Sometimes, when you look at the challenges confronting you, you see many, not one. You see the "sword and spear and shield" rather than the resources of God. Sometimes your battles can be won with the simple things you hold in your hands—a mission, a calling, a commitment, and an opportunity. As you know, "With God, nothing is impossible."

> "So David triumphed over the Philistine
> with a sling and a stone;
> without a sword in his hand
> he struck down the Philistine and killed him."
> (1 Samuel 17:50)

> "In God's word he said 365 different times,
> 'Do not fear.' Now, if he says it that
> many times, you know he's
> serious about it, don't ya?"
> Mark Richt – Football Coach

Heavenly Father, you know I don't like fights. And I didn't choose the battle that faces me right now. On the surface, the opposition is greater than the human support behind me. It looks like I may be alone in this. But I know I am never alone when I follow your lead. So I commit again to you my humble resources. Take them and use them as you will. I will leave the results with you. In the name of Heaven's Champion I pray. Amen.

Forgive Me, Please—I was Wrong

Have you ever had someone say to you, "I'm sorry…I was wrong. Please forgive me"?

If you have heard those words, you probably remember the "who—when—why—and where." In living color and surround sound! Human forgiveness is an unforgettable way to correct a wrong done against another person. And if you had to say those words to someone else, you will remember that moment forever.

Seeking forgiveness from another person doesn't always go as planned. But seeking forgiveness from God is never an exercise in futility. It is a spiritual blessing. The Apostle John said, "If we confess our sins (to God), he is faithful and just to forgive us our sins and to cleanse us from all unrighteousness."

(1 John 1:9).

Honest, sincere confession to God results in sins forgiven. Today. Always. Forever.

"I—yes, I alone—am the one who blots out your sins for my own sake and will never think of them again."
(Isaiah 43:25 NLT)

"If I have wounded any soul today;
If I have caused one foot to go astray;
If I have walked in my own willful way,
Dear Lord, forgive!

If I have uttered idle words or vain;
If I have turned aside from want or pain;
Lest I myself shall suffer through the strain,
Dear Lord, forgive!

Forgive the sins I have confessed to Thee;
Forgive the secret sins I do not see;
O guide me, love me and my keeper be,
Dear Lord. Amen."

Lyrics by C. Maude Battersby

Father in Heaven, I can never thank you enough for your mercy and grace. Most of all, Father, I praise you for forgiving me of my past sins. Satan remembers each one of them and is quick to remind me of my transgressions. But you, Lord, have forgotten each one of them, and you have promised that you "will never think of them again." I will always glorify your name for that. Amen.

Get Your Spiritual Eyes Checked

When was your last eye exam? This year? Last year? Can't remember? You may be overdue.

When did you last ask God to open your spiritual eyes to the needs of people around you? Can't remember? You may be overdue there as well.

Eye exams usually take about an hour, after which you are good to go. A spiritual eye exam may take more planning and more effort on your part. Are you ready? Great! Here is your assignment.

Set aside an hour and go to a shopping mall, or a park, or a fast-food place—pick one. Find a place to sit where you can watch people, and then pray this very simple prayer: "Father, help me to see people the way you see them. Amen."

That's all there is to it. Then sit back and let God correct your vision. God definitely will answer a prayer like this. Directions will come. The Holy Spirit will help sharpen your vision for other people. And you may discover that you are never "good to go." The quality of your new vision may surprise you.

"Let each of you look not only
to his own interests,
but also to the interests of others."
(Philippians 2:4)

"I alone cannot change the world.
But I can cast a stone across
the waters to create many ripples."
Mother Teresa

Heavenly Father, it is so easy for me to close my eyes and heart to others, especially to strangers. Being self-centered is a characteristic of the secular mind. But that outlook runs counter to the example of Jesus. Open my eyes to the real needs of others, to the end that I can become more Christ-like. In His Name I pray. Amen.

Give and You Will Definitely Receive!

It's a principle of life. Give generously, and you will receive generously. Give grudgingly, and you will cheat yourself out of a blessing. Don't give at all, and you will be the loneliest person in town.

Ebenezer Scrooge learned the lesson the hard way, didn't he? But he recovered in time to receive a blessing only Tiny Tim could give—respect, and unbelievable love. A major department store in the east came up with a promotional pitch during a Christmas sale.

"Buy More, Save More. Free Shipping."

I think I understand the "free shipping" angle, although I know that somebody will pay for it. What I don't understand is how I can save more by spending more. Whenever I see those words I want to reply, "Sorry. I can't afford to save any more this year."

But you can receive something by giving. In fact, the more you give, the more you will receive. Jesus said it, so it must be true. And there's even more. Don't you love the "good measure, pressed down, shaken together, and running over" idea? And best of all, it will be poured into your lap. You don't have to go out looking for it. It will find you.

"Give, and gifts will be given you.
Good measure, pressed down, shaken together,
and running over, will be poured into your lap;
for whatever measure you deal out to others
will be dealt to you in return."
(Luke 6:38 NEB)

"Give what you have.
To someone, it may be better
than you dare to think."
Henry Wadsworth Longfellow – American Poet

Heavenly Father, I confess that I can't explain very well the concept of Grace. Except that I know it is not a promotional gimmick. These are tough times, Lord. Money is tight everywhere. Economists tell us to hold-on rather than give-away. But I know of no better cause to support than the Kingdom of God. Suffering is happening everywhere in the world. Help me to give generously, and begin by laying on my heart the things and people that are on your heart. I promise I will be generous. Because it's the right thing to do. Amen.

God Hears Prayers—Even Short Ones

There are no short prayers in the Bible. But if there were, would God answer them? Of course! And will he answer your short prayers? Absolutely!

Jesus wanted his disciples to know that long prayers were no more valid than short prayers. No buildup time was necessary. In fact, in Matthew 6:7 Jesus warned his followers against adding a lot of repetition to their prayers. In the prayer that Jesus encouraged his disciples to follow, he used only fifty words. Some churches repeat that prayer every Sunday as part of their liturgy.

There is an expression motion-picture directors use to encourage script writers to get to the point without wasting time. "Cut to the chase!" Can that apply to the prayers that you address to God? Of course! Our Father knows what we need before we ask, and he is already preparing an answer. How good is that?

"And when you pray,
do not use vain repetitions as the
heathen do, for they think
that they will be heard for their
many words. Therefore do not
be like them. For your Father
knows the things you have need of
before you ask Him."
(Matthew 6:7, 8)

"For God is in heaven, and you on earth;
therefore let your words be few.
For a dreamcomes through much activity,
and a fool's voice is known
by his many words."
(Ecclesiastes 5:2, 3)

"Be sincere. Be brief. Be seated."
Franklin Delano Roosevelt

Father in heaven, I'll be brief. You know what my needs are. I believe you are already at work in my behalf with a timely response. I rest on your integrity. I trust in your Word. I just want to say today that I will honor your wisdom in whatever you allow to come my way, because you know what is best for me. Please accept my humble praise for the ways you have helped in the past and for the ways you will continue to help me today and in the future. This prayer comes straight from my heart. Amen.

God Is With You
Nothing Else Matters

Have you ever been alone in a dark place, where even if you cried out, no one could hear you? Here is Frank's story.

Walking home late one night following work, Frank decided to take a shortcut through a neighborhood cemetery. He couldn't see in the dark, and he accidently stumbled into an open grave that had been dug in preparation for a graveside service the next day.

Frank was not injured, but he was alone. He tried to climb out, but the hole was too deep. He called out for help, but no one answered. Finally, he decided to make the best of his situation until morning, when he was sure someone would come along. He sat down in one corner of the grave and tried to get some sleep.

Later that night, another man—taking a shortcut through the same cemetery on his was home—stumbled into the same grave. He assumed he was alone; he didn't realize someone else had fallen into the grave ahead of him. And, like Frank, he tried every way he could to climb out of the hole, without success.

Finally, from his spot in the corner of the grave, Frank spoke up: "Mister, you ain't ever going to get out of this hole."

But he did! And if you are in a dark place alone, there's hope for you. God is near. Trust him.

> "So do not fear, for I am with you;
> do not be dismayed, for I am your God.
> I will strengthen you and help you;
> I will uphold you with my righteous right hand,"
> (Isaiah 41:10)

> "What gives me the most hope every day is God's grace;
> knowing that his grace is going
> to give me the strength for whatever I face,
> knowing that nothing is a surprise to God."
> Rick Warren

Heavenly Father, my heart is encouraged when I reflect on the fact that nothing is a surprise to you. You know the end from the beginning. You know what my decisions will be, before I announce them. And when I end up in a tight, dark place, you know the way out. Your Word teaches me to not fear. With your help, that is exactly the course I will follow. Amen.

God Keeps His Promises--Always

When God makes promises, he keeps them. Every one of them. How does he do this? Haddon Robinson observed that God keeps his promises to his children in three ways:

• **Miraculously**. The Lord removes the problem miraculously.

• **Empoweringly**. The Lord empowers us to accomplish even the most difficult tasks.

• **Patiently**. The Lord gives us the grace to live through the hard challenges of life.

In the Old Testament the word used most for a solemn promise is the word "covenant." The Hebrew word for covenant means "a solemn agreement with binding force." Marriage, therefore—in a biblical sense—is not a contract. It is a covenant in that it is a sacred agreement between a man and a woman regarding themselves. When God makes a covenant with someone, it is irrevocable and eternal—everlasting!

How is the Lord helping you deal with the difficulties that you are facing right now? Is he at work eliminating the source of your troubles? Is he at work in empowering you to do things that are far beyond your natural abilities and talents?

Or is he whispering to you, "My grace is sufficient for you?" However he does it, he keeps his promises. Once he has promised you something, you can count on it.

> "Understand, therefore, that the Lord your
> God is indeed God. He is the faithful God
> who keeps his covenant for a thousand generations
> and lavishes his unfailing love
> on those who love him and obey his commands."
> (Deuteronomy 7:9 NLT)

> "Of all the promises we make and break,
> perhaps the most tragic are those we make to God.
> And yet we keep promising,
> for whom else can we turn to in times of real crisis?"
> Pamela McQuade

Father, give me ears to hear what the Spirit is saying, and then give me the grace and courage to accept his promises by faith—considering them done. And help me be a blessing to those who are listening to the wrong voices. Remind me that part of my job is to point others to Jesus, the Source of all truth. In the powerful, never-changing, eternal name of the Promise Keeper, I pray. Amen.

God Really Cares About You

Have you ever wondered if God knows where you live? Have you ever asked yourself, "Is God too busy to notice me?" Have you ever mused, "Does God even know my name?"

David, the psalmist knew. The shepherd David knew. The musician David knew. The kid with the five smooth stones and home-made sling—that David knew. David, the slayer of Goliath of Gath, knew. David, Israel's second king, knew. Courageous warrior David knew. The same David who coveted Bathsheba, the wife of one of his loyal soldiers—he knew. David, who prayed, "Search me, O God, and know my heart; test me and know my thoughts. Point out anything in me that offends you, and lead me along the path of everlasting life." That David knew.

In Psalm 139:13 David said, "You made all the delicate, inner parts of my body and knit me together in my mother's womb." David had no doubt at all about how much God knew and cared about him.

Why is it that we doubt so much and worry about this and that? If David was right, God is watching us in the same way he watched King David. And he likes what he sees. Rejoice! Tell somebody today.

> "O Lord, you have examined my heart
> and know everything about me.
> You know when I sit down or stand up.
> You know my every thought...
> How precious it is, Lord,
> to realize that you are thinking about me constantly
> ...And when I wake up in the morning
> you are still with me!"
> (Psalm 139:1-2; 17-19 NLT)

> "Before God created the universe,
> he already had you in mind."
> Erwin W. Lutzer

Father God, I am humbled when I think about your love for me. Just reading the words written thousands of years ago by King David brings tears to my eyes. I am unworthy of your mercy, but you offer it to me over and over again. Accept my praise and thanks. If you are willing, allow me the opportunity to return your love to me with a renewed dedication to your cause. In the strong name of Jesus I pray. Amen.

God's Grace Is The Thing for You

Do you know anyone who has had successful lens-implant surgery? In most cases their lives have been completely changed—for the good.

Eye cataracts develop over time. Almost imperceptibly the eyes adjust to the cloudiness that keeps the full light of reality from being seen. But there is a problem. A person with cataracts can't see true colors. Bright sunlight causes annoying glare. Corrective lenses do not correct the problem. Surgery will.

Only a visually-impaired person can appreciate the before-and-after-difference successful lens-implant surgery makes. People who were near-sighted for most of their lives can now see distant objects without corrective lenses. Colors that were muted prior to surgery become bright. It is an awesome experience.

Life has a way of "clouding" or diffusing the pleasures that should accompany your everyday experiences. Good things may come your way, but you may be so distracted that you simply can't see clearly. But God can make the difference. Grace is what you need.

The problem may be that you may be reluctant to ask for God's grace. You may think his grace is for other people, and not for you. And you would be wrong. God's grace is for everyone. Accept it today.

> "Even though on the outside it often
> looks like things are falling apart
> on us, on the inside, where
> God is making new life,
> not a day goes by without
> His unfolding grace."
> (2 Corinthians 4:16 MSG)

> "Prayer does not change God,
> but it changes him who prays."
> Soren Kierkegaard – Danish Philosopher

Lord God. I want to accept your grace in my life. Help me to not be distracted by things that seem to be falling apart, but to look to you in faith. Reveal to me where you want to engage in my life, and let me praise you with every bit of strength I have. In the strong name of Jesus I pray. Amen.

Halloween Revisited

Have you ever wondered how Halloween got its name? If you were a child again, your answer might be, "For all the scary outfits kids wear." But you would be wrong. It has nothing to do with outfits!

In 837 A.D., a Roman Catholic leader—Pope Gregory III—initiated a celebration to honor Christian martyrs. He called it call it "All Saints Day"—November 1. The evening before the feast of celebration, October 31, was celebrated as "All Hallows' Eve"—Halloween.

On the Eve of All Saints Day in 1517, an Augustinian monk and parish priest named Martin Luther nailed a list of 95 questions to the door of the Castle Church in Wittenberg, Germany. These questions set off a revival of the reading and teaching of the scriptures in Germany and beyond. The Protestant Reformation was born.

Among the many hymns Luther wrote, "A Mighty Fortress" is perhaps the best known. The words he used to describe God—Mighty Fortress, Bulwark, Helper—have been sung around the world, in multiple languages, for five hundred years.

The Psalmist said, "He is my refuge and my fortress; my God, in Him I will trust." When you next sing Luther's great hymn, be reminded that God still is mighty, a bulwark never failing! Hallelujah!

> "He is my refuge and my fortress;
> my God, in Him I will trust."
> (Psalm 91:2)

> "A mighty Fortress is our God, a Bulwark never failing;
> Our Helper He, amid the flood of mortal ills prevailing.
> For still our ancient foe doth seek to work us woe;
> His craft and power are great,
> And, armed with cruel hate, on earth is not his equal.
> And though this world, with devils filled,
> should threaten to undo us,
> We will not fear, for God hath willed
> His truth to triumph through us.
> The prince of darkness grim—we tremble not for him.
> His rage we can endure, for lo, his doom is sure;
> One little word shall fell him."
> Martin Luther

Father God, I want to thank you and praise you for the miraculous way your Word—once limited to reading and study by scholars—became available to the world through men like Martin Luther, who also wrote hymns for public worship. My prayer is that the words of Luther's hymn might resonate in my heart and soul. And Father, accept my worship and praise as I think about the many ways you are my refuge—keeping me safely out of harm's way. Amen.

Happiness Is Everything It's Cracked up to Be

Martin Luther spoke about Christians having a "great and quiet heart." He was speaking about an attitude with which a person should approach life and living.

A "great heart" is not a lazy heart. It is a joyful heart —a heart with an attitude that says, "You can do this, and you can be joyful in doing it." A "quiet heart" is not a passive heart. It is a heart with a settled confidence. It has a calm sense of direction that resists distractions.

Jester Hairston was one of the most dynamic composers/arrangers of black spirituals of the 1950s and beyond. In one setting he combined a particular spiritual with a traditional hymn.

"Come Thou Fount of every blessing, Tune my heart to sing Thy grace; Streams of mercy, never ceasing, Call for songs of loudest praise."

To this hymn Hairston added an upbeat chorus with a new, non-traditional, spiritual rhythm: "I say it's all over me and it's keepin' me alive, keepin' me alive, keepin' me alive; Yes, it's all over me and it's keepin' me alive, King Jesus is keepin' me alive." Just thinking about it should make you want to dance.

"Those who listen to instruction will prosper;
those who trust the Lord will be happy."
(Proverbs 16:20 NLT)

"Never be careful or anxious,
but commit all to Him,
and live in serene tranquility;
with a great and quiet heart,
as one who sleeps safely and quietly."
Martin Luther

Heavenly Father, I have never considered happiness to be an entitlement, but I have thought of it being a byproduct of a life consecrated to you. I don't deserve it, Lord, but I want it. Lead me there; direct me in how I may attain it. Let me sing with the choir, "Yes, it's all over me and it's keepin' me alive, King Jesus is keepin' me alive." Amen.

Help Is on the Way—Be Encouraged

Doug was hospitalized for treatment of acute weakness. No cause was obvious. He was kept for several days while multiple tests were administered. Doctors eventually figured it out. Meds were prescribed. Problem solved. Don't you wish all problems could be solved that simply?

In the hospital, Doug was assigned to a private room. Nurses came by periodically to check his vital signs—more frequently at night than during the day when he was awake. One nurse was particularly annoying. She used an expression that experienced patients learn to suspect whenever they hear it said. She said, "I'll be right back." Maybe she forgot—or got busy. She did not back up her words with action. Doug was never a patient in that hospital again.

How different with God. When he says, "I'll be right back," that's the way it will be. And when he says, "Help is on the way," you can count on him to show up. Every time. But God wants us to be faithful in doing everything we can do to follow his instructions, just as we hope God will be faithful in doing everything we ask him to do for us. Help may not show up within the time frame we want, but help is coming! As the psalmist said, "Expect God to get here soon." He will.

> "Be brave.
> Be strong.
> Don't give up.
> Expect God to get here soon."
> (Psalm 31:24 MSG)

> "Never give in, never give in,
> never, never, never, never—
> in nothing, great or small,
> large or petty—never give in,
> except to convictions of
> honor and good sense."
> Winston Churchill

Father, I have observed that bravery always seems to work in movies—where a script writer describes a brave action, and the actors act it out. But being brave and courageous in real life is no easy matter. King David had no trouble being brave, except when he was tempted beyond his ability to make the right moral choice with Bathsheba—the wife of Uriah, an officer in Israel's army. David must have been speaking from experience when he wrote Psalm 31—especially verse 24. Father, let this verse be your Word to me. But I need your help to carry out the directions. I look to you now for help. Amen.

Hope Is No Small Thing—It's Huge

Some Christians believe that wealth and health in this life are entitlements for believers, and bad times are automatic for unbelievers. Do you believe that stuff? Let's talk about that concept.

The truth is that bad things happen to some very good people, and some very bad people seem to be among the most successful people on earth.

The Bible teaches that while pain and sorrow may be part of life here on earth, God offers hope to the faithful. And best of all, all disappointment will disappear one day when you see Jesus. For now, however, you can be hopeful. As the title of a song suggests, "My Times Are in His Hands." Every single minute. Every single hour. Every single day. And, as the words of another song read, "It will be worth it all, when we see Christ."

Enthusiasm is not listed in the Bible as a spiritual gift, but perhaps it should be on your "bucket list" to pursue. Enthusiasm might not cure anything, but it may make your friends happy to see you practice it. Give it a try.

> "So, my dear brothers and sisters,
> be strong and steady, always enthusiastic
> about the Lord's work,
> for you know that nothing
> you do for the Lord is ever useless."
> (1 Corinthians 15:58 NLT)

> "Hope is being able to see that
> there is light despite all the darkness."
> **Bishop Desmond Tutu**
> South African Civil Rights Leader

> "We must all accept finite disappointment,
> but we must never lose infinite hope."
> Martin Luther. King, Jr.
> American Civil Rights Leader

Heavenly Father, I accept for myself the affirmation the Apostle Paul wrote to the Church at Corinth. When disappointment comes my way, I will not complain. I will remain steady. I will continue praying and believing until I more clearly see your hand in the events of my life. Help me to hold on to that hope, even when other people lose hope in the face of disappointment. Amen.

How Secure Is Your Faith?

Have you ever wondered about how secure you were in your belief in God? Join the club.

The Apostle Paul knew that some believers in the Church at Rome were concerned about issues like these. In Chapter 8 he answered their questions.

Paul was not taking the position that it is impossible for people to lose their salvation once they yielded their lives to Jesus. He did not say that nothing in all creation can separate you from God.

He said that nothing can separate you from the love of God. This means that God will love you throughout your entire lifetime. He will not give up on you. He will keep pursuing you until your ability to respond to him no longer exists.

Joining a church and reciting the Apostles Creed will not save anyone. Reciting marriage vows will not guarantee a successful marriage. Both require conditions to be met. God's conditions never change! Neither has he changed his mind about you. Celebrate that!

> "And I am convinced that
> nothing can ever separate us from his love.
> Death can't, and life can't.
> The angels can't, and the demons can't.
> Our fears for today, our worries about tomorrow,
> and even the powers
> of hell can't keep God's love away."
> (Romans 8:38 NLT)

> "I know not what the future hath
> Of marvel or surprise,
> Assured along that life and death
> His mercy underlies."
> John Greenleaf Whittier

Heavenly Father, the national news media always seem to spin the day's happenings in a way to create unrest and anxiety. No wonder Americans hold the media in such disregard. A secular mindset is a negative mindset. Your Word provides a positive balance to truth, and it offers hope to those who trust in God. In spite of being in prison, the Apostle Paul had great news for the Christians in Rome, and for us. He proclaimed that nothing can ever separate us from your love. I rely on that truth today. Amen.

It's Okay to Draw a Line in the Sand...and Stand

American history contains numerous stories about leaders who became legendary by challenging their followers to fight to the death to defend a righteous cause. It's called "drawing a line in the sand."

The phrase is commonly associated with the Battle of the Alamo. Colonel William Travis, who commanded the Alamo defense forces, was faced with the reality of being totally annihilated by the forces of Mexican General Antonio Lopez de Santa Anna. His soldiers had surrounded the American defenders, and Santa Anna demanded full surrender.

Travis assembled his defenders, explaining to them that defeat was a certainty. Then he reportedly pulled his sword, drew a line in the sand and asked for volunteers to cross over and stand with him. Most did. Badly outnumbered, they fired their cannons in defiance of the call to surrender, and the battle raged. "Remember the Alamo" became a battle cry that has inspired soldiers from that time until the present. Worldliness and godliness are not compatible. The question Moses asked of Israel still calls for an answer: "Who is on the Lord's side?" Cross over the line and stand for the right. Don't settle for less.

> "Stop loving this evil world
> and all that it offers you,
> for when you love the world,
> you show that you do not have
> the love of the Father in you."
> (1 John 1:15 NLT)

> "Worldliness is an attitude, a spirit,
> an atmosphere that permeates
> the whole of human society.
> It is an attitude that puts self first and
> ignores God and His commandments.
> Its horizon is this present
> world, and it never gives a thought
> to God or to eternity."
> Dr. Billy Graham

Heavenly Father, I pledge to stand with you. I've seen the other side, and I cannot stand there. I know there will be setbacks and sorrow, pain and possibly persecution for those who follow Jesus, but I like what is in store for all who are faithful to the end. As Luther said, "Here I stand; I can do no other." Amen.

It's Time to Sing Again

In his opening devotional of *Morning and Evening* Charles Spurgeon said, "We are ordained to be the minstrels of the skies; let us rehearse our everlasting anthem before we sing it in the halls of the New Jerusalem."

Anyone can repeat the secular sounds of the irreligious. Being negative is an easy road to follow. Choose any headline hawked by the main-stream media and be depressed. Their notes are mostly sorrowful.

But that is not the song God wants you to sing. His song is joyful and hopeful. The lyrics of the gospel ring with optimism and gladness. God wants you to look up, not down. He wants you to advance, not retreat.

He wants you to look ahead to what has not yet been written, not backward to the pain and failures of the past. He wants you to "shout aloud to the Rock of our salvation," and be thankful.

> "Come, let us sing for joy to the Lord;
> let us shout aloud to the Rock
> of our salvation. Let us come
> before him with thanksgiving
> and extol him with music and song."
> (Psalm 95:1-2)

> "We will be glad and rejoice in You.
> We will not open the gates to the sorrowful
> notes of the organ, but to the
> sweet strains of the harp of joy
> and the high-sounding
> cymbals of gladness."
> Charles H. Spurgeon

Heavenly Father, each Lord's Day is an opportunity to celebrate your goodness and love. Help me to forget the difficulties of the past and remember them no more. Lift my sights to see what you see for me. Give me the voice to sing a song of joy to you, and give me the energy "to shout aloud to the Rock of our salvation." I want to be "a minstrel of the skies" to everyone you send across my pathway. I am dedicated to that mission. In the Name of the Lord Christ I pray. Amen.

Jesus Did It All—for You

There is a mentality that is popular today, but it is as far from being true as night is from being day. It goes something like this:

"I am what I am today because of what I have accomplished in life." William Barclay calls this "a soliloquy in the first person singular."

God is nowhere to be found in this way of thinking. It is the "I did it my way" mentality. It is the "I'm up here and you are down there—get over it" syndrome.

That might play well in the boardroom, but it doesn't play at all where life is really lived. And when it comes to salvation, it doesn't equate at all. Salvation is all of Jesus and none of you.

You paid no price for your salvation. Not one penny. It was a gift of God. As the apostle said, it was all of grace, "not of works, lest any man should boast." (Ephesians 2:9)

Rejoice and be glad!

> "That's what Christ did definitively:
> suffered because of others' sins,
> the righteous One for the unrighteous ones.
> He went through it all—
> was put to death and then made alive—
> to bring us to God."
> (1 Peter 3:18 MSG)

> "Jesus came to our world so
> that he could take us to his."
> Author Unknown

> "Well, you say that He died;
> And what you say is so;
> But don't you see He rose again?
> That's what you've got to know.
> He prayed and cried and went and died,
> Did all that He could do.
> And I believe that Jesus
> Did it all for you."
> Dallas Holm – Christian Vocalist

Heavenly Father, in my heart I know I have done nothing to deserve your mercy. It was all of your grace. My 'works' had nothing to do with it. I know my happiness as a Christian is dependent on my relationship with you and my interrelationship with others. More than anything else I want you to reign in my life. I surrender my past and present to you. I ask that you shape my life into something resembling yours. In the strong name Jesus I pray. Amen.

Jesus Will Help You Now

You may remember the story. The man was physically challenged. We don't know how he got that way. We know nothing about his parents, or even his name. Everything changed the day Jesus met him.

Jesus had a question for him. "Do you want to get well?" Jesus was looking for a one-word answer: "Yes" or "No."

Instead, the man offered an excuse: "Sir, I have no one to help me into the water when the water is stirred. When I am trying to get in, someone else goes down ahead of me." Jesus reckoned that a "Yes."

At the very most, the man was hoping Jesus would help him into the pool the moment the bubbles started riseng to the surface. Nothing more than that. All he wanted was a helping hand down into the healing pool. Instead, he got a helping hand up into health and life.

Do you need that kind of help? Perhaps you need to lift your sights from the crippled world around you and discover the world God sees for you. It is bigger and more beautiful than you ever imagined.

Perhaps you need to watch for the slender man in the white robe with the question that will change your life. He's the one who asks, "Are you willing to put yourself into my hands? The answer he is looking for is a simple "Yes." *Now* will work for him.

> "When Jesus saw (the crippled man)
> lying there and learned that
> he had been in this condition
> for a long time, he asked him,
> 'Do you want to get well?'"
> (John 5:6 NLT)

> "It's all over me and it's keepin' me alive,
> keepin' me alive, keepin' me alive.
> Well, it's all over me and it's keepin' me alive.
> King Jesus is keepin' me alive!"
> Traditional Spiritual

Heavenly Father, I confess I like to do things my way. But I have learned through experience that when I insist on doing things my way, you step aside and let me do them. And too often my way is the wrong way. Help me to learn from my mistakes. Help me to seek your will and your way, rather than insist on my own. And let me recognize your hand reaching down to lift me up. That is the path I want to follow. Amen.

Let God Light Up Your Life

Thomas Edison was a world-class inventor and scientist. He may have had more ideas than all the other inventors that preceded him—put together. During his lifetime he was responsible for the creation of nearly eleven hundred patents.

Edison saw many of his experiments fail, but he continued doing them. Thousands of times! He knew it was better to get up than to give up. He set an example for everyone who is committed to excellence. Even you!

In his search for a long-lasting filament for what he eventually called the "light bulb," Edison experimented with hundreds of fibers and metals. In 1879 he discovered a method for making an inexpensive filament that would handle the stress of electric current. Today we would call his discovery "carbonized cotton fiber" thread! But the filament was so fragile that it easily broke. Almost by accident, he tried inserting the filament into an oxygen-free tube. To his surprise, the filament glowed! It didn't burn long, but it burned.

In the Christian life, you may face many stumbles and failures. The voice that seems loudest is not the voice of the Father, but the voice of the Adversary.

He doesn't whisper, "Nice try." He shouts, "Failure!" It's the Other Voice that you want to hear. That Voice says, "My strength is sufficient for you." God wants to reward you for your achievements—not condemn you for your failures. Rejoice!

> "For though a righteous man falls
> seven times, he rises again…."
> (Proverbs 24:16 NIV)

> "Many of life's failures
> are people who did not realize
> how close they were to success
> when they gave up…
> I have not failed.
> I've just found 10,000
> ways that won't work!"
> Thomas A. Edison

Heavenly Father, sometimes I feel like it is easier to accept failure than to continue pushing for success. Then I see the Cross, and I realize the price that you paid to make me your child. Help me stay the course. Let me see the crowd of witnesses that line my pathway, encouraging me. Most of all, let me see Jesus. Let me feel his hands reaching out to steady me. Help me to understand he wants to stand beside me, live within me, lift and boost me as I obey his Word. In his strong name I pray. Amen.

Life's Number One Question

According to one Internet source, there are approximately 3,300 questions in the Bible. Some are theologically significant. Some are not. Some are rhetorical. Some are meant to entrap, accuse, ridicule. Not all of them are equally important.

But there are a few that stand out. Two in particular—one in the Old Testament; one in the New.

The Old Testament question was asked by the prophet, in Micah 6:8. The question: "What does God require of you?" He answered in three short phrases—"Act justly—love mercy—walk humbly with your God."

The New Testament question was more complex. It was addressed to Jesus by a young Jewish lawyer. The lawyer asked, "Which is the most important commandment in the Law?"

The question was not new. It had been debated by Jewish scholars for centuries, and it was thought to be a question no one could answer. The lawyer was wrong. He asked for one answer; Jesus gave him two. Plus a powerful comment. The discussion was over.

The answer was, "Love God—Love Others." Could the question really be answered that simply? Jesus said it. It must be true.

> "Teacher, which is the most important
> commandment In the law of Moses?
> Jesus replied, 'You must love
> the Lord your God with
> all your soul and all your mind…
> A second is equally important:
> Love your neighbor as yourself.
> All the other commandments
> are based on these two commandments.'"
> (Matthew 22:37-39)

"No worse fate can befall a person in this world
than to live and grow old alone,
unloving and unloved."
Henry Drummond

Heavenly Father, keep me from making the gospel too complex. Help me to understand that your plan for me is to love you and love others. Help me to keep it simple. Help me to keep it practical. Help me to keep it personal. Help me to understand the central truth of the gospel: Jesus died to save sinners and to prepare them to spend eternity with him in heaven. To this end, use me to tell others. Amen.

Living Upstream in a Downstream World

Nearly every American who loves literature has heard of Walden Pond in Concord, Massachusetts. It is famous because of one person—Henry David Thoreau, who lived there for two years around 1845.

But have you ever heard of Whitman's Pond in Weymouth, Massachusetts? Probably not. The pond is remembered, not because of a famous person who resided there years ago, but because of a fish—a species known as alewives—or Atlantic herring. And not just a few of them. How about a half-million alewives that spawn there in April of each year?

As they have for more than four centuries, hundreds of thousands of small herring will leave their natural habitat in the Atlantic Ocean and instinctively fight their way upstream against the prevailing downstream current to Whitman's Pond. These herring have a singular purpose—to create a new generation of baby herring before returning to the sea themselves.

A Christian's purpose in life is much different than a herring's purpose.

But the commitment to fight against the downward drift of our secular culture is very much the same. As David Jeremiah observed, "We can't escape our culture, but we don't have to be shaped by it."

> "Enter by the narrow gate;
> for the gate is wide and the way is easy
> that leads to destruction,
> and those who enter by it are many.
> For the way is hard that leads to life,
> and those who find it are few."
> (Matthew 7:13-14 RSV)

> "The current of our culture is
> downward, and many people
> just drift along with the moral flow.
> Living for Christ is like
> rowing upstream."
> David Jeremiah

Heavenly Father, help me to be a singular-minded Christian. Keep me from following the path of the double-minded. Lead me to the Cross of Jesus, and let me follow Him to the Crown that awaits all believers who persist until they reach their Spirit-directed destination. Amen.

Look Up, Not Down

C.S. Lewis once said, "A proud man is always looking down on things and people; and, of course, as long as you're looking down, you can't see something that's above you."

And what are some of the things that are above you? Plenty. Trees, hills, mountains, clouds, sky. And God, of course. There is an old saying that reads,

"If within you there is nothing above you, you will eventually surrender to everything that is around you."

That's true, isn't it? We all know people who have surrendered to things and habits that exist at a lower level than where they really want to live. But we also know people who have surrendered to a higher calling, to a higher purpose, to a higher way of living —the way that Jesus talked about when he walked on earth. You probably know people who have invested in noble causes. They are people who have discovered a divine source of help. They have discovered that—like the psalmist—their help "comes from the Lord, the Maker of heaven and earth." You can be like them.

"I lift up my eyes to the hills—
where does my help come from?
My help comes from the Lord,
the Maker of heaven and earth."
(Psalm 121:1-2)

"I can see how it might be possible
for a man to look down
upon the earth and be an atheist,
but I cannot conceive
how he could look up into the heavens
and say there is no God."
Abraham Lincoln

Father God—Maker of heaven and earth, Creator of mountains and valleys, Designer of streams and lakes and oceans, Composer of the greatest music ever written, Poet who inspired hymn writers of past generations, Singer of the Psalms, Spirit of all true believers, Savior of the World —I can't begin to praise you enough for what you have done to lift my sights above the things that are going on around me. Plant within my heart a passion to know you fully, to obey you completely, and to strive to be like you in everything I do. Amen.

Make Winning a Habit

Question: Can you tell the difference between confidence and arrogance? Hint: they are not the same.

The Apostle Paul was not arrogant when he wrote to the Church at Philippi. He was, however, confident. He was conscious of his human weaknesses, but he knew the source of his strength. He knew that through Christ he could accomplish whatever God called him to do.

How unlike today's culture! You live in a day in which secular achievements are celebrated by receiving awards and being voted into halls of fame. Paul, on the other hand, took a humble route.

He said, "When I am weak, then I am strong" (2 Corinthians 12:10). He took no credit for the victories God had allowed him to enjoy, even though he experienced some powerful ones.

Are you willing to do the same, by acknowledging your weaknesses and giving God the praise for your achievements? You can make a habit of doing so.

> "I can do all things
> through Christ
> who strengthens me."
> (Philippians 4:13 NKJV)

> "We are conscious of our own weakness
> and of the strength of evil; but not of the
> third force… the habit of victory…
> which is at our disposal if we will
> draw upon it. What is needed is a
> deliberate and whole-hearted
> realization that we are in Christ,
> and Christ is in us by His Spirit."
> Bishop Charles Gore
> English Social Reformer

Heavenly Father, as I evaluate my personal strengths and gifts in relationship to the demands of the work to which you have called me, I fall short. My weaknesses are greater than my strengths. On my own, I will probably fail. It is only as I submit to your Lordship in my life that I will experience victory. So, I surrender to you today. I will repeat this process tomorrow. And the days following. I pray that as I do this, you will develop in me the habit of victory. Through Jesus Christ I pray. Amen.

Miracles Still Happen Today

Do miracles still happen today? Short answer: Yes. Even when skeptics disagree? Yes. Does faith enter into such things? Often.

In biblical times, leprosy was a disease that was shrouded in superstition and fear. People with leprosy were declared "unclean" by society, and these disenfranchised victims were required to announce their disease whenever they came near healthy people. Jesus changed all of that.

Jesus wasted no time in correcting a life-threatening malady. He prayed no public prayer. He made no attempt to discover the source of the man's problem. He saw the need, heard the man's sincere plea, and he healed him. Instantly.

But that was then. This is now. What may have been impossible fifty years ago has changed due to scientific discoveries and new medical procedures. Is there still a need for miracles today? Ask those suffering. Does God perform miracles today? People of faith believe he does.

Are there things that cripple you? Do you desperately need a miracle in your life? Ask God now. Then believe.

> "A man with leprosy came and knelt
> in front of Jesus, begging to be healed.
> 'If you want to, you can make me well again,'
> he said. Moved with pity, Jesus touched him.
> 'I want to,' he said. 'Be healed!' Instantly
> the leprosy disappeared—the man was healed."
> (Mark 1:40-41 NLT)

> "That hand which multiplied the loaves,
> which saved sinking Peter,
> which upholds afflicted saints,
> which crowns believers—
> that same hand will touch every seeking
> sinner, and in a moment make him clea."
> Charles H. Spurgeon – Clergyman

Lord, your Word teaches me to ask, to seek, to knock. This story is a reminder that you are willing to grant my requests, but you want me to ask. So, Lord, I am asking. Look past my failures and see the person you want me to be —better than the person I am now. You did it for the leper; I know you are able to do it for me. Thank you for giving me hope that you will do what is needed to set me free from everything that drags me down. Amen.

Never Lose Hope! Good Always Wins

Is the Old Testament character, Job, on your list of favorite biblical characters? He should be—especially if you or anyone you love has overcome major personal setbacks. Job is on my list.

When did Job live? We don't know, but it was a very long time ago—probably around 2000 B.C. Scholars tend to agree that he lived after the Great Flood.'

Job had a right to complain. He lost everything of tangible value within the course of one day. He was wealthy and had a large family—in his era, a sign that God was pleased with him. He had extensive lands, possessions, and flocks so enormous that he was set for life. In addition, the Scriptures say that he was "blameless and upright." Imagine that!

According to the biblical account, Job's integrity became the subject of a cosmic debate between God and Satan. As a result, in Round 1 Job lost his ten children, livestock, and servants. In Round 2 he was afflicted with gross body sores. His wife even urged him to curse God and die.

But Job did not lose hope. Eventually hope won. Job became the standard of moral excellence for generations to come.

"For I know the plans I have for you,"
says the Lord. "They are plans
for good and not for disaster,
to give you a future and a hope.
In those days when you pray,
I will listen. If you look for me
in earnest, you will find me
when you seek me. I will be
found by you," says the Lord.
(Jeremiah 29:11-14a, NLT)

"Hope is the thing with feathers
That perches in the soul
And sings the tune without words
And never stops at all."
Emily Dickinson, American Poet

Heavenly Father, I can't begin to imagine the human anguish Job experienced in the loss of health, family, and possessions. But my heart rejoices when I reflect on his courage, determination, and integrity. By comparison, my complaints are few. And when I face disappointment, I am encouraged to push back and keep hope's light burning brightly. Thank you for reminding me of this grand truth and the story behind it. Amen.

Out-of-this-World Grace

Good—Better—Best—Amazing. They are called "modifiers." They help you grade certain variables of life—everything from tires to seats in airplanes. Here are four modifiers and their synonyms:

- **Good**: Average, Standard, Regular, Normal, Expected, Bronze-medal-winner, Coach Class
- **Better**: Mid-range, Above-average, Unexpected, Silver-medal-winner, Business Class
- **Best**: Excellent, Superior, Top-flight, Outstanding, Gold-medal-winner, First Class
- **Amazing**: Incredible, Superior, Unequaled, Off-the-charts, Unbelievable, Out-of-this-world

Amazing describes God's grace: Unmerited, Unequaled, Astonishing, Awesome, Unique

In his book, *In the Grip of Grace* (Word Publishing, 1996), Max Lucado told a story about being on a plane and seated next to a fourteen-year-old named Billy Jack. The boy introduced himself to Lucado by saying, "Good, I'm glad you're sitting by me. Sometimes I throw up." What a way to begin a flight! Lucado concluded, "I remembered Billy Jack. He would have understood the idea of grace. He knew what it was like to place himself totally in the care of someone else."

Grace is placing yourself totally in the care of God who created the universe. That is why we call it "Amazing."

> "For it is by grace you have been saved,
> through faith—and this not from
> yourselves. It is the gift of God—
> not of works, so that no one can boast."

> "Isn't it amazing that tears and rain alike
> can cleanse the stain that living brings,
> and leave all fresh and bright?
>
> Isn't it amazing that a Savior from above
> came to earth to save our souls,
> because of holy love?
>
> Isn't it amazing that each is given free,
> the tears, the rain, the saving grace?
> God gave them all to me."
> Gael Phaneuf

Heavenly Father, I don't ask for wisdom to understand your grace. I ask for courage to celebrate it. I ask for patience as I learn how to place myself totally in your care. I ask for your forgiveness for my being so slow in doing so. And I ask for faith to accept your grace as you offer it to me without reservation. In the Name of the Giver of Grace I pray. Amen.

Perseverance Is Not for Babies

Alonzo Mourning is a name well-remembered by professional-basketball fans as one of the greatest defensive centers of all time. During his 15-year National Basketball Association career, "Zo" was perennially named to the NBA All-Defensive Team and was twice named Defensive Player of the Year.

In 2003 Mourning retired from basketball due to a serious kidney disease. But later that year he received a life-saving kidney transplant from a cousin. Within a year Mourning was back in playing shape and eventually signed a free-agent contract with the Miami Heat. In 2006 he and his team won the NBA Championship. Mourning is a prime example of the saying, "Perseverance is not for babies!"

Perseverance is a powerful virtue. The best achievers in sports at any level learn very early-on how to overcome adversity on their way to major accomplishments. Do champions ever fail in their efforts to achieve? Most certainly, yes. Are they content with failure? Never. Is perseverance a good word to describe the serious follower of Christ? Absolutely!

> "Blessed is the man who perseveres under trial,
> because when he has stood the test,
> he will receive the crown of life
> that God has promised to
> those who love him."
> (James 1:12 NIV)

> "It is defeat that turns bone to flint;
> it is defeat that turns gristle to muscle;
> it is defeat that makes men invincible.
> Do not then be afraid of defeat.
> You are never so near to victory as
> when defeated in a good cause."
> Henry Ward Beecher
> American Clergyman and Social Reformer

Heavenly Father, I want to excel in the things I do. I am not thrilled when trials come my way. It is hard for me to accept them as part of your will for me, although deep in my heart I know that you have allowed them to come to me. I pray for strength and courage to persevere until the trial is over. May those watching me be encouraged by what they see. And may your name be praised for allowing all of this to happen. Amen.

Pursue God – He's Pursuing You

Do you know that some people are convinced the Christian world can be divided into two groups—those who pant after God and those who *rant* about him for whatever reason? Think about it.

The psalmist was clear in terms of which group he belonged to. He was thirsty for God in the same way that a deer thirsts for water. Unquenchable thirst. Never-satisfied thirst. Even risking-death-to-find-it thirst.

Do you remember hearing preachers challenging a congregation with these words? "You can have as much of God as you want." As a teen I thought that was stupid. Then I met Mrs. Widmark. Now there was a woman who could never get enough of God. When she said, "Let's pray about it," she was not mouthing some worn-out phrase. She really meant that she would engage in earnest prayer until an answer came.

> "As the deer pants for the water brooks,
> so my soul pants for You, O God.
> My soul thirsts for God, for the living God."
> (Psalm 42:1 NIV)

> "God—you're my God! I can't get
> enough of you! I've worked up
> such hunger and thirst for God,
> traveling across dry
> and weary deserts."
> (Psalm 63:1 MSG)

> "Longing, longing for Jesus,
> I have a longing in my heart for Him;
> Just to be near Him, to feel His presence,
> I have a longing in my heart for Him."
> Richard Baker

> "Of course the will of God is the same for all.
> He has no favorites within His Household.
> All He has ever done for any of His children
> He will do for all of His children.
> The difference lies not with God, but with us."
> A.W. Tozer —Christian Minister/Author

Father, create in me a greater thirst for you. I am not satisfied with an occasional thirst. I want a daily—a passionate—thirst for you. I don't want a second-hand thirst, or an artificial thirst. I want a thirst that I sense when I awaken in the morning and when I close my eyes to sleep at night. The psalmist longed for this experience because you put it in his heart to ask for it. I am asking that you put it in my heart as well. In your Son's name I pray. Amen.

Push Back Against Negative Thinking

Is there such a thing as the power of negative thinking? You know there is! Read the Opinion Page of your daily newspaper. Or watch the Nightly News on T.V.

Negative thinking is alive and well in the world. But it doesn't have to be. You can make it disappear. How can you do that? By exercising the power of positive thinking and by inviting Jesus to be the Lord of your life.

Is there a valid source where both positive and negative thinking can be found—along with guidelines for overcoming the bad thinking of today? Absolutely! It's right there in the Bible—God's Holy Word. Any translation will do.

The Apostle Paul understood that bad things happen to good people. But he understood that when Christ lives within you, he helps you not only to survive, but to overcome the negativity of the times in which you live. The enemy of your soul tries to get you to believe that negativity is inevitable. Nonsense. The Devil lies.

> "In general and in particular I have
> learned the secret of facing either
> plenty or poverty. I am ready for
> anything through the strength
> of the one who lives within me."
> (Philippians 4:12-13 -- Phillips)

> "Don't surrender leadership of your life to negative facts,
> negative faces, negative fears—or a negative faith."
> Robert H. Schuller
> Minister, Writer

Lord, I want to be ready for anything that comes my way. I cannot do this in my strength alone. I must have your presence living within me. I am tired of living under bondage to negative influences and pessimistic people. I surrender them to you now. In faith I affirm that God is able to do what is needed to lift me above the challenging circumstances of life. In the powerful name of Jesus I pray. Amen.

Put Your Pedal to the Metal

No professional baseball player played with greater dedication and intensity than former Kansas City Royals star George Brett. Throughout his career he gave all that he could give to become a Hall-of-Fame player.

In a pre-retirement interview Brett was asked what he wanted to do in his last at-bat before retiring from baseball. The three-time batting champion replied,

"I want to hit a routine grounder to second and run all out to first base, then get thrown out by a half step. I want to leave an example to the young guys that that's how you play the game—*all out.*"

The Christian life is not for the faint-hearted and the lazy. It is a demanding life that calls for a full commitment to go all out to be the best that you can be. If you follow the example of Jesus and will go anywhere, do anything, and give your very best in service to him, you will be a champion someday. It is in losing your life that you will find it, and it is denying yourself that you will develop the skills needed to follow closely after Jesus.

"Then Jesus said to his disciples,
'If any of you wants to be my follower,
you must put aside your selfish
ambition, shoulder your cross,
and follow me. If you try to keep your
life for yourself, you will lose it.
But if you give up your life for me,
you will find true life.'"
(Matthew 16:24-25 NLT)

"My mantra has always been
to have zero regrets in life.
Everything I do at one speed.
I go all-out."
Appollo Ohno
Olympic Speed-Skater

Heavenly Father, I know there is a price to pay to become a champion. I have known people who have tried to find short-cuts to success in their moral and spiritual lives, and they have failed. I not only want to be a spiritual success, but I also want to be an example of excellence to those who look up to me. I don't want to be a 'loser' in life, unless it is losing myself in service to Jesus Christ. Thank you for pushing me to become authentic in my faith as a follower of the True Champion, Jesus Christ. Amen.

Reach Out to Jesus–He's Very Close

A woman was in distress. She had spent years and nearly everything she owned in a futile effort to find a cure for her disease. She was desperate. Hope was nearly gone. She was determined to get close to Jesus. She thought, "If I could just touch him—how could there be any harm in that?"

As Jesus passed by, the woman reached out and brushed her hand against his robe. Immediately, the bleeding stopped. The pain was gone. Her withered muscles felt like new.

Jesus turned to the crowd that followed him and asked, "Who touched me?" His eyes searched the faces. His disciples were not sympathetic. One of them said, "All this crowd is pressing around you. Everyone has touched you!" But Jesus persisted. Finally the woman moved toward the Master, and fell at his feet. Jesus said to her, "Daughter, your faith has made you well. Go in peace."

Are *you* hurting? Do you feel unnoticed? You are not unnoticed by Jesus. He feels your touch when you reach out to him in faith. If the touch of an anonymous woman in a crowd can get the attention of the Lord of glory, will he not do the same for you? Good! Reach out to him now. Believe.

"And suddenly a woman who had a
flow of blood for twelve years
came from behind and touched the hem
of His garment; for she said to herself,
'If only I may touch His garment,
I shall be made whole.'
But Jesus turned around,
and when He saw her He said,
'Be of good cheer, daughter;
your faith has made you whole.'
And the woman was made
well from that hour."
(Matthew 9:20-22)

"He is always there, hearing
every prayer, faithful and true
Walking by your side, in his love
we hide, all the day through
When you get discouraged,
just remember what to do
Reach out to Jesus,
he's reaching out to you."
Ralph Carmichael

Heavenly Father, thank you for noticing me, even though others around me may ignore me. Help me to muster faith to believe that you not only hear my plea, but that you love me and want to answer my prayer. I am reaching out to you now. Thank you for answering my prayer today. Amen.

Really Great News— Better than You Think

Have you ever wondered if there were a simple, straight-forward passage of Scripture that leaves no doubt about God's eternal Plan of Salvation? Get ready. Your question has been answered.

In his epistle to the Church at Rome, the Apostle Paul offered a glimpse of God's Plan of Salvation. Chapter 8 begins and ends with the best news anyone can find in terms of a person's relationship with God.

Verse 1 begins with the affirmation that there is *no condemnation* for those who belong to Christ Jesus. And the chapter ends with the affirmation that there is *no separation* from the love of God.

Powerful. No condemnation and no separation. Have you ever read greater assurances in the New Testament? Claim this affirmation for yourself, by faith.

> "I am convinced that nothing
> can ever separate us from his love. Death can't,
> and life can't. The angels can't, and the demons can't.
> Our fears for today, our worries about tomorrow,
> and even the powers of hell
> can't keep God's love away.

> Whether we are high above the
> sky orin the deepest ocean,
> nothing in all creation will ever
> be able to separate
> us from the love of God
> that is revealed in
> Christ Jesus our Lord."
> (Romans 8:28-29 NLT)

> "Could we with ink the ocean fill
> And were the skies of parchment
> made,Were every stalk on earth
> a quill,And every man a scribe
> by trade, To write the love
> of God aboveWould drain
> the ocean dry,Nor could the scroll
> contain the whole, Though
> stretched from sky to sky."
> Frederick Lehman

Heavenly Father, the national news media always seem to spin the day's happenings with fear and anxiety. A secular mindset is a negative mindset. Yet your Word not only provides a positive balance to truth—it offers hope to those who trust in God. In spite of being in prison, the Apostle Paul had great news for the Christians in Rome. He proclaimed that nothing could ever separate me from God's love. I rest on that truth today. Amen.

Relax: God's Timing Is Always Perfect

Old sayings, like old houses, seem to have a life of their own. Some are restored by a younger generation and come alive again. Here's an old saying for you to consider. "God never hurries, but he is never late."

Maybe you saw the message someone posted on Facebook:

> **"God has perfect timing.**
> **It takes a little patience.**
> **And a whole lot of faith.**
> **But it's worth it."**

Have you discovered the Message translation of the Bible? Here's a new rendition of an old affirmation by the prophet Micah in 7:7. "But me, I'm not giving up. I'm sticking around to see what God will do. I'm waiting for God to make things right."

God's perspective is timeless. He functions without a time zone. Location is important to realtors, but not to God. The seriousness of our situation may trouble us, but not him. Wherever you are today, God is watching.

One thing is definite. God will show up—in his time. But at your place. He knows what is best for you, and he will make sure things turn out according to his plan—and always on time. Keep the faith, and let God take charge of everything else.

> "But these things I plan won't happen right away. Slowly, steadily, surely, the time approaches when the vision will be fulfilled. If it seems slow, wait patiently, for it will surely take place. It will not be delayed."
> (Habakkuk 2:3 NLT)

> "With God, when nothing's happening, something's happening."
> Reuben Welch
> Minister/Teacher

Lord, teach me the importance of trusting in your timetable. I know you have a perfect timetable for me, and I know I don't have a voice in determining what it is. That's fine with me. When it's right for me to know, I am confident that you will reveal it to me. In the meantime I will watch for the signs and the direction you want me to take.

Right or Wrong—It's Up to You

Around 6 a.m. on Sunday morning, August 27, 2006, a tragic event took place at Blue Grass Airport in Lexington, Kentucky. Comair commuter jet Flight 5191, scheduled to fly to Atlanta and carrying 50 on board, attempted a takeoff on a wrong runway and subsequently crashed and burned. Forty-nine persons on board died.

Commenting on the tragedy, another airline captain said, "Assumed truth had crept into the cockpit." The captain continued, "Situation awareness was lost, and attention to the very basics of flight departures was compromised." People died because of pilot error.

Writer Renda Brumbeloe, himself a former airline pilot, concluded, "We live in an age where absolutes are disdained in the public square. To be right, we must keep relative values out of our lives, out of our churches, and out of our beliefs. What we believe and practice matters."

Are there some "absolutes" in your life to which you are unquestionably faithful? Are your values measured by God's Word? Or the Culture? Do others around you know what you stand for, without compromise? The choice is yours. Be careful.

> "There is a way that seems
> right to a man, but its
> end is the way of death."
> (Proverbs 14:2)

> "If you don't know
> where you're going, you're
> probably going wrong."
> Sir Terrance Pratchett
> British Writer

Heavenly Father, the Kentucky story is another reminder that there are some absolutes in life that cannot be disregarded or postponed. I realize my decisions are often impulsive and premature. But I know the Controller, and he knows where I am. I need to follow the guidelines that have been set out for me. I pray that you will help me carefully weigh decisions that may harm me and cripple others. Today I yield my will to you. In the strong Name of your Son I pray. Amen.

Seek the Simple Life
People Will Love You for It

You probably won't recognize the name given him by his mother, but you may remember the name he chose for himself, and for which church history remembers him—Brother Lawrence. He became famous—not for worldly achievements—but for something quite unexpected. His thoughts.

He was born Nicholas Herman in the first decade of the 17th Century in France. But his writings are as current as today's.

In mid-life he entered a monastery in Paris where for 15 years he worked as a cook for the religious community of over a hundred men. He had no great love for kitchen work, but he approached it with the same level of commitment and discipline with which he approached every assignment given to him.

He lived a life that was uncomplicated and simple. It was only after his death that his writings were discovered and eventually printed in a book, *The Practice of the Presence of God*. The influence of his writings is immeasurable. Here is what he said about his walk with God:

"I walk before God simply, in faith, with humility and with love; and I apply myself diligently to do nothing and think nothing which may displease Him…and this without any other view than purely for the love of Him, and because He deserves infinitely more."

> "Well done, good and faithful servant:
> you were faithful over a few things,
> I will make you ruler over many things:
> enter into the joy of your lord."
> (Matthew 25:21 NKJV)

> "A simple life is not seeking how little
> we can get by with—that's poverty—
> but how efficiently we can put first things first.
> When you're clear about your purpose and
> your priorities, you can painlessly discard
> whatever does not support these…."
> Victoria Moran
> American Writer and Speaker

Heavenly Father, I confess that my attitude toward the work you have given me has not always been perfect. I was hoping for success in many things, while you were looking for faithfulness in a few things. I was hoping to reach the top, while you were looking to see how well I performed at the entry level. I longed for respect, while you were looking for signs that I could enable others to earn respect for the things they did. I am not a finished product; I need your help to improve the quality of my life and work. Help me to follow you in faith, with humility and with love. Amen.

FRIDAY—Absolutely the Best Day of the Week

A news reporter asked a man a question about his job. The question was, "What do you like best about work?" The man answered, "A paycheck." There you go. No hesitation. Just an honest answer.

During most of her years of full-time employment, Janie didn't receive a paycheck per se. Her pay was electronically transferred to her bank account. Paydays came and went, and life pretty much stayed the same.

However, what Janie liked most about work were not paychecks and pay days, but Fridays. The pace remained about the same, but the focus changed. Plans were made for the weekend. Goodbye work; hello everything else. She loved working, but she really loved Fridays.

Janie is retired now, and she reports that every day is like Friday. Not quite heaven, but close. For a Christian, any day is a good day to rejoice and be glad. But Fridays are especially nice.

While you are thinking about it, how about thanking God for the blessing of a job? And Fridays!

"This is what the Lord says:
'Heaven is my throne,
and the earth is my footstool.
My hands have made both
heaven and earth, and they
are mine. I, the Lord, have spoken!'"
(Isaiah 66:1-2 NLT)

"This is the day the Lord hath made;
He calls the hours His own;
Let heaven rejoice, let earth be glad
And praise surround the throne."
Isaac Watts

Heavenly Father, I want to say that because of you, my life has been enriched. Your involvement in the work I do and the decisions I make causes me to rejoice. In my mind I picture myself kneeling in front of your throne, and my heart is overcome with joy. Thank you for walking with me today—lifting, encouraging, healing, and helping. Today is special because of that. Every day is special because of that. I praise your name right now. Amen.

Take a Second Look at Eternal Things

Have you heard about an internet gathering that refers to itself as "The Church of What's Happening Now—the First Church of Reason"?

Cute. Do you suppose they give credit to Flip Wilson, the comedian who introduced the church name on his television show in 1970? America loved Flip in his role as Reverend Leroy. One can only guess what America thinks of the current "reverend" of the YouTube production.

You live in a world dominated by the Now senses—feeling, seeing, hearing, smelling, tasting. Immediate stuff. The secular world wants you to believe that these are the only things by which reality can be experienced. Today's world has no interest in what eternity is. But you do—don't you?

Lorado Taft (1860-1936) was one of the most distinguished American sculptors of the early 20th Century. One of his criticisms of modern art was that the "precious hint of eternity which is sculpture's greatest asset has been completely eliminated." What he said about the art of his day could be said of almost everything being sold by some religions to the public today. Eternity is missing.

The Apostle Paul had it right. Christians should fix their eyes on the *unseen*, not just on what is seen—not on the temporary, but on the eternal. In fact, eternity should be part of everything you do—wherever you attend church.

> "So we fix our eyes not on
> what is seen, but on
> what is unseen.
> for what is seen is temporary,
> but what is unseen is eternal."
> (2 Corinthians 4:18)

> "If we build to please ourselves,
> we are building on the sand;
> if we build for the love of God,
> we are building on the rock."
> Oswald Chambers
> Scottish Clergyman

Heavenly Father, forgive me for spending so much time and effort on the *now* things of life, rather than on the *later* things of life. Help me to focus on things with heaven in view. Remind me to set my priorities on things that last—not on things that rust. Help me to keep my eyes on Jesus, "the author and finisher of our faith." In his strong Name I pray. Amen.

Temptation—No Sin in That

As a teen growing up in a small, conservative, evangelical church, Billy didn't have college-educated Sunday School teachers. They were older ladies, very sincere and deeply devoted to God. He loved every one of them. But there was a problem.

Most of the theological knowledge of Billy's Sunday School teachers was pretty much limited to the preaching of the pastor and the itinerant evangelists who came to town each year to hold a Revival. The pastors who served during Billy's teen years were college-trained, but few of the paid evangelists had attended college. The church was not big enough to afford a paid youth minister. So, Billy's understanding of temptation led him to believe that temptation itself was a sin, that unless regularly confessed (at the church altar in front of everyone)—needed to be avoided at all cost. Billy feared he would forever be identified by the desires that every teenage boy experiences.

When Billy was in his mid-teens, a new minister was invited to become his pastor. He had a son about Billy's age, and the new pastor understood kids.

He preached the truth, including helping Billy understand that every human being that ever lived—including Jesus—faced temptations of every kind. Billy's concept of temptation was changed forever. Yours can be changed as well, beginning today.

> "No test or temptation that comes your way is beyond the course of what others have had to face.
> All you need to remember is that God will never let you down; He'll never let you be pushed past your limit; He'll always be there to help you come through it."
> (1 Corinthians 10:13 MSG)

> "Temptation is the devil looking through the key hole. Yielding is opening the door and inviting him in."
> Billy Sunday
> American Evangelist

Heavenly Father, when I think about complaining to you about the temptations I face, I am reminded that I am not the only person in this world to suffer duress. More importantly, remind me that God himself is the source of my strength, and through his Spirit he will bend every effort to rescue me—often in the nick of time. Thank you for reminding me of this truth. Amen.

The Darker the Night, the Brighter the Stars

Sam was a kid in 1942 when the song, *Deep in the Heart of Texas*, topped all popular songs on the Billboard charts for weeks. Eight years later Sam was in San Antonio, Texas, where he saw in person what the lyricist wrote about in her opening lines,
"The stars at night are big and bright."

Sam was born and raised in Southern California, where the city lights in the Los Angeles basin were so bright at night that one needed a telescope to enjoy the brightness of the stars. But when Sam enlisted in the United States Air Force and was assigned to Lackland Air Force Base in Texas, he came to understand what the lyrics of that song really meant.

The parade grounds at Lackland were huge, and at night when all the parade ground lights were turned off, one couldn't see anything but stars—big and bright. What made the stars appear so visibly bright? Darkness.

In the life of a Christian—most people face times when the darkness of pain, loneliness, disappointments, and failures obscures the light that Jesus brings. Darkness is everywhere and is much to be avoided. But must it be?

"Jesus said to the people,
'I am the light of the world. If you follow me,
you won't be stumbling through the darkness,
because you will have the light that leads to life.'"
(John 8:12 NLT)

"Only in the darkness
can you see the stars."
Martin Luther King, Jr.
Civil Rights Leader

"I like the night. Without the dark,
we'd never see the stars."
Stephanie Meyer –
American Writer

Heavenly Father, the world without Christ is a very dark place to be—day or night. But because of the light your Son brought to the world 21 centuries ago, there is enough light for anyone who seeks Him. I am so glad I sought him when I was a child. I am also thankful for those who mentored me during my teen years. Without Jesus, the world would be a dark place—a place without stars to bring me hope. I praise you today, Father, and the One you sent to be "the light of the world." Amen.

The Power of the Human Touch

Irish author Alexander Irvine (1863-1941), in his book *My Lady of the Chimney Corner*, told of his sainted mother, Anna. She was one of those humble Christians who took on everyone's burdens as if they were her very own.

One day a neighbor lady came to see Anna. It was obvious the neighbor was in deep distress. She said to Anna, "I can't make it through the day, Anna, unless I receive a fresh touch of God." Anna suggested that they kneel and pray together for that touch from God. They knelt side-by-side and began to pray together. As they did so, Anna reached out her hand and placed it on the woman's head. In a few minutes, as they concluded their prayer, Anna asked, "Did He touch you?" The woman replied, "Oh, yes, Anna. I felt His hand—but it felt strangely like your hand."

Anna quickly responded, "It was my hand, but it was God's hand too. Sometimes God takes the hand of a bishop; sometimes God takes the hand of a surgeon; and sometimes G0d takes the hand of a poor old creature like me. It was my hand, but it was His hand, too!" Then Anna said,

> "Christ takes a hand wherever He can find it."

What a powerful truth that is! Our hands are Christ's hands. Our voice is Christ's voice. Our love is Christ's love. Our touch is Christ's touch. We are instruments of God's grace. The Apostle Paul understood this well when he wrote to the Christians at Rome,

> "We have different gifts,
> according to the grace given us.
> If a man's gift is prophesying,
> let him use it in proportion to his faith.
> If it is serving, let him serve;
> if it is teaching,
> let him teach; if it is encouraging,
> let him encourage;
> if it is contributing to the needs
> of others, let him give generously;
> if it is leadership, let him govern
> diligently; if it is showing mercy,
> let him do it cheerfully."
> (Romans 12:6-9 NIV)

Heavenly Father, I offer my hands to you today. Use them as you will. If through them you are able to bring comfort to others, your Name will be praised. Make me to be sensitive when I am around those to whom you want to minister. Amen

Turn It Over—To God

Noel Stookey is a singer-songwriter-guitarist who became famous in the 1960s as a member of the folk-music trio, "Peter, Paul, and Mary." Noel assumed the stage-name "Paul" because it had a better ring than "Peter, Noel, and Mary."

In the fall of 1979, Stookey performed a solo concert at a college in Oklahoma. He entertained a packed auditorium of students and fans from Kansas, Texas, Arkansas, and Oklahoma. During the concert he introduced one of his songs, "Turn It Over," by telling how farmers prepare the soil for planting, and the importance of "turning over the soil" as part of the process.

> "Deep in the woods the sound of an axe
> Clearing a field by the sweat of his back
> A man of the soil plants his seeds
> And prays that the earth will provide his needs.
>
> Turn it over—to the Father
> Turn it over—to the Son
> Turn it over—to the Spirit,
> Until the Kingdom come."

Are you troubled by things that seem impossible to correct—by setbacks in your family or business—by disappointments connected with your church? All are very hard things. Maybe it's time to "turn it over" to the Lord. As the psalmist said:

> "Give your burdens to the Lord,
> and he will take care of you.
> He will not permit the
> godly to slip and fall."
> (Psalm 55:22 NLT)

> "God will never leave you empty.
> He will replace everything
> you lost. If he asks you
> to put something down, it's
> because he wants you
> to pick up something greater."
> Author Unknown

Heavenly Father, I bring my problems and concerns to you today. I don't know where else I can leave them. Your word teaches me to cast my burdens on you, for you care for me. Help me do that now, I earnestly pray in the Name of the Father, and the Son, and the Spirit. Amen.

Angels Are Everywhere

An unplanned encounter between an elderly couple and the manager of a small hotel in Philadelphia turned out better than anyone could imagine. It happened years ago on a cold, rainy night in the city. The couple inquired at the desk, "Can you possibly provide us with a room for the night?" The manager's name was George. His reply was, "Sorry, Sir. The hotel is full. All rooms are taken."

George's hands were tied. But it was well past midnight, and he did not want to send the couple out into the stormy night. So he said, "Would you perhaps be willing to sleep in my room here at the hotel? I am working all night anyway, and I won't get to bed until tomorrow." The couple accepted the offer and rested comfortably that night in the manager's personal room.

When checking out the next morning, the elderly guest said to George, "You are the kind of manager who should be the boss of the best hotel in the United States. Maybe someday I'll build one for you!" Both men laughed, but the one making the suggestion was serious.

Several years later, George received a letter from the elderly gentleman, inviting him to come to New York City for a weekend. A round-trip ticket was enclosed. When George arrived, there was a car waiting for him, and he soon reached his destination—the corner of

Fifth Avenue and Thirty-fourth Street, directly in front of a brand-new hotel, a splendid structure of reddish stone. Joining him at the curb was the gentleman he had helped years earlier. "This," the gentleman said, "is the hotel I have just built for you to manage." The manager's was George C. Boldt. His benefactor was William Waldorf Astor, and the hotel—the most famous of its day—was the Waldorf-Astoria Hotel.

Watch for those angels. They are everywhere!

> **"Be ready with a meal or a bed when it is needed. Why, some have extended hospitality to angels without ever knowing it."**
> (Hebrews 13:2 MSG)

> **"We should treat well all strangers who seek our help. Under a ragged coat they may hide their wings!"**
> Fulton Oursler

Heavenly Father, help me be sensitive to everyone that crosses my path. It is so easy to look away from strangers when they pass by me. Encourage me to look them in the eye and greet them warmly. They may be people you have sent to me—people who need encouragement or other things I can provide. I don't want to miss an opportunity to be a blessing. Thank you for bringing this truth to my attention. Amen.

Whatever You Do—Do It Well

In the Old Testament story of the Exodus, God really didn't want a temple. He was doing just fine with tents. In fact, there was a time when God accompanied the Hebrews in a pillar of fire. That was cool.

No matter how awesome the idea of a temple might be, people would look at it and say, "Maybe God is in there." But if God's people were to see a pillar of fire, that would be something special. And if the pillar was rising up within reach of the leader when he said, "Believe in God," people would say, "Okay."

The Children of Israel insisted on a temple. So God said, "Okay, but if you're going to build it, you're going to use the best materials in the world—you're going to make sure it's the most awe-inspiring building anywhere. And it's going to cost you!" Again, God didn't need a temple. But if the people wanted a temple, he insisted it had to be extraordinary.

God always drives his people towards excellence. He created you to be free and creative. But he has a built-in standard. He wants you to do whatever you do with excellence! And he wants you to be the best that you can be.

> "Whatever is noble…
> right…pure…lovely…admirable—
> if anything is excellent or praiseworthy—
> think about such things.
> Whatever you have learned or received
> or heard from me, or seen in me—
> put into practice."
> (Philippians 4:9)

> "Excellence is a better teacher
> than mediocrity. The lessons of the
> ordinary are everywhere.
> Truly profound and original
> insights are to be found
> only in studying the exemplary."
> Warren G. Bennis
> Business Pioneer

Heavenly Father, many of the people in my world seem content to be average—to be common. They approach life with a survivor mentality, not with a champion mentality. They don't cry out to be excellent—they are satisfied to just get by. But your call is a call to be praiseworthy. And that is my goal. I want to be the best that I can be—as a husband, as a dad, as a grand-dad, as a friend, as a servant. Keep before me a dream of doing my job well. Not for my glory, but for yours. In the strong name of Jesus I pray. Amen.

You Are Special—Never Forget That

Do you remember a time in your childhood when the kids chose sides for a pick-up game at school, and one kid never seemed to be chosen? Cedric was one of those kids.

In grade-school Cedric was tall, gangly, slow in a foot race, and not athletic at all. He was always there—hoping to be picked by a team. And he grew to be tall. So tall he could no longer be ignored by his fellow students.

By the time he reached high school, Cedric had grown to be a foot taller than any boy in school. Athletically, Cedric was a project—but he was seen as a potential center who could win every jump ball. Eventually, Cedric got to choose the players around him.

KidsHealth says that healthy self-esteem is "a child's armor against the challenges of the world...Kids who feel good about themselves seem to have an easier time handling conflicts and negative pressures." Patterns of self-esteem begin early in childhood and last well into adulthood.

Do you consider yourself to be somebody special? Excellent! God does, too. You are special to him.

> "For you are a people holy to the Lord your God.
> The Lord your God has chosen you
> out of all the peoples on the face of the earth
> to be his people, his treasured possession."
> (Deuteronomy 7:6 NIV)

> "Every person in the world is hungry.
> Yes, every person in this world is hungry for
> something, be it recognition, companionship,
> understanding, love—the list is endless."
> John C. Maxwell –Developing the Leader within You

> "I know I'm somebody,
> 'cause God don't make no junk."
> Ethel Waters – Gospel Singer

Heavenly Father, sometimes I struggle with self-doubt. It's hard to look at myself and feel totally good about what I see. I know my faults; they stand out in my mind above my abilities. But in my heart I know you believe in me. I tend to see my problems; you see my potential. Lift my sights to the level of your expectations for me. Help me to see myself as you see me—your treasured possession. Amen.

You Can Be Number One

On October 15, 2002, the Associated Press reported that the Dallas Cowboys had honored the distinguished life and ministry of Dr. Billy Graham by presenting him with a Cowboy jersey with the name GRAHAM on the back and the number "1" in large print on the front and back. Dr. Graham responded to the presentation in a way that demonstrated his unique sense of humor.

"It has my name on the back and says I'm No. 1. I may show up at the next game and see where they put me."

Was Dr. Graham serious? Of course not! But he had the right idea. Everybody longs to be a champion, or at least root for a team that has a chance to be Number One.

Spiritually speaking, there's a jersey somewhere with your name on it. It may not say "Number 1" on the front and back, but it's your size. You have been chosen. The Lord Himself has called you. He wants you to show up at the next game. How about doing just that? You might be surprised to see where in the game he puts you. You may be a starter!

> "But you are a chosen people,
> a royal priesthood, a holy nation,
> a people belonging to God, that you may declare
> the praises of him who
> called you out of darkness
> into his wonderful light."
> (1 Peter 2:9)

> "You have been chosen, and you must therefore use
> such strength and heart and wits as you can."
> J.R.R. Tolkien
> English Writer and Poet

Father, I tend to see myself through the eyes of others—family, friends, associates. I want to please them in what I do. If they decide I should be in the stands rather than on the field, I accept that. If they expect me to be a backup player, that will work for me. I don't have a jersey with my name on the back. And if I did, the number would not be "1." Forgive my short-sightedness! Help me to see myself as you see me, not as others see me. Give me the courage to believe that there is a task out there that I can do. I'm ready to go. Point me in the right direction. I'm checking in! Amen.

You Can't Fly without Wings

Have you ever heard the story of how professional basketball star Bill Russell overcame the fear of failure? Fear affects everyone, but you hardly expect a six-foot, ten-inch professional basketball player to be anxious about failure.

According to one source, after every game Bill graded his effort on a scale of one to one-hundred. Reflecting back on his career, Bill said he never achieved more than a grade of sixty-five. If that were true, some observers would conclude that Bill Russell was only an average basketball player.

Instead, Bill played in twelve hundred professional basketball games and was subsequently inducted into the Professional Basketball Hall of Fame.

By Bill's personal evaluation, some would say he never achieved his goal of excellence. Yet it was striving for that goal that made him one of the greatest men ever to play the game.

Continually striving for excellence is what it takes to be a champion in any endeavor. Make that your personal goal in life. Begin now.

> "He gives strength to the weary
> and increases the power of the weak.
> Even youths grow tired and weary,
> and young men stumble and fall;
> but those who hope in the Lord
> will renew their strength.
> They will soar on wings like eagles…."
> (Isaiah 40:29-31 NIV)

> "We are not meant to trudge
> sadly along as victims
> of our problems.
> God has equipped us
> with wings to soar
> above them."
> Dr. David Jeremiah
> American clergyman

Heavenly Father, I need to meditate on Isaiah's wisdom. I am prone to grade myself against what I see in others. Instead of praying for wings to soar, I have a tendency to ask for a rope to grip and survive life's challenges. Lift my sights higher, Lord. Give me courage to pursue lofty goals. In the strong name of Jesus I pray. Amen.

You Have What You Need—Enjoy It

There is an old saying that suggests that Guilt is concerned with the past, worry is concerned about the future, but contentment enjoys the present. Is that how you look at life? If so, we are on the same page.

Some years ago a psychologist conducted a survey among a group of adults. The question he asked was, "What do you live for?"

He discovered that the vast majority said they simply were enduring the present while they waited for something better to happen down the road. Only 6 percent of those surveyed said they considered their present relationships or activities were reasons for living.

How sad. I wonder how many Christians were included in that survey.

Experience is a reliable teacher. It helps you evaluate the past, and it also equips you to face the challenges of today.

You can learn to be content. The Apostle Paul had a lot to say on the subject. Check it out.

"Don't worry about anything;
instead, pray about everything.
Tell God what you need,
and thank him for all he has done.
If you do this,
you will experience God's peace,
which is far more wonderful
than the human mind can understand."
(Philippians 4:6-7 NLT)

"During the years since time began,
Today has been a friend of mine;
But in his blindness and his sorrow,
he looks to yesterday and tomorrow.
Forget past trials and your sorrow.
There was, but is, no yesterday,
And there may be no tomorrow."
Author Unknown

Heavenly Father, Teach me how to enjoy the present to the full. I get tangled up when I try to correct the past, and I am frustrated when I try to take care of tomorrow's problems today. Keep me focused on what I can handle today. I know that will lead me to your peace, for which I thank you in advance. Amen.

Give Flowers that Will Never Die

Flowers, like all living things, eventually die—unless they are artificial, of course. Cut flowers die in a few days or a week. Flowering plants may last months. But all flowers die. Nevertheless, Americans annually spend millions of dollars on flora and fauna, and florist shops keep busy year-around, even in the dead of winter.

With absolute certainty about the zero survival-rate of cut flowers, customers keep buying them, arranging them, displaying them, touching them, smelling them, watering them, and then—sadly—discarding them when they are wilted. The most sentimental among us press them and keep them permanently between the pages of a book or diary.

Why do people buy flowers? They do it to remember, to celebrate, to honor, to mourn. Even though they know these multi-colored tokens of love will soon have to be discarded, they still buy them and give them. Flowers help celebrate a life, a memory, a major event, a commitment, a landmark decision.

Have you ever thought about sending special flowers to persons you love or admire? Not flowers that will eventually die, but flowers that will never die—word pictures that keep on living in the hearts and minds of the recipients for months and years?

King David was the greatest word flower giver of all time. His psalms were his legacy to the nation. Stories about David are found in several books of the Old Testament. But his stories are word snapshots of victory and defeat. His writings are something else; they became his gift in perpetuity. They have lasted thousands of years and have been read by millions. Why? Because they are a beautiful record of his spiritual pilgrimage. Open any of his songs and you will see flowers. How about this one from Psalm 16:5 and 6 (NIV):

> **"Lord, you have assigned me**
> **my portion and my cup;**
> **you have made my lot secure.**
> **The boundary lines have fallen**
> **for me in pleasant places;**
> **surely I have a delightful inheritance. . . .**
> **The Lord is my light and my salvation—**
> **whom shall I fear? The Lord is the stronghold**
> **of my life—of whom shall I be afraid?"**
> Psalm 27:1-2 (NIV)

Don't you wish you could write word pictures like that? You can. There are people who need to hear an encouraging word from you. And when you write to someone in your own handwriting, your words will be keepers. And unlike flowers, your words will never die.

Never Underestimate the Power of Two

Israel's King David selected a group of soldiers he called his "Mighty Men." The most famous warrior of them all was Josheb-basshebeth. He personally took on 800 of the enemy, "whom he killed in one encounter." (2 Samuel 23:8) Outstanding!

Next in order of fame was Eleazar. He fought alongside David when the Philistines gathered for battle at Pas-dammim. But most of David's men retreated in fear of the Philistines, leaving David and Eleazar to stand alone against the enemy. The record shows that Eleazar "stood his ground and struck down the Philistines until his hand grew tired and froze to the sword." (2 Samuel 23:10)

Eleazar swung his sword with so much determination that his hand muscles froze up. But note the next line: "The Lord brought about a great victory that day." God made the difference.

Eleazar gave all that he had, and more. But it was not enough. The battle was the Lord's! How unlike some of today's world leaders, who love receiving personal credit for their successes. Eleazar had a job to do, and he did it. But when his strength waned, the Lord added *his* strength to the warrior's strength and secured the victory.

Perhaps the most interesting thing about this story is that Eleazar wasn't alone. King David stood with him. And the Lord stood with both of them. In life and work you don't always get to choose your battlefields. They may choose you, or they may just come with the territory—the commitment you made when you hired on. You may be able to handle some of the challenges. Others are too great for you alone. Where does your additional strength come from? The psalmist knew. He said,

> "My help comes from the Lord,
>
> the Maker of heaven and earth."
>
> (Psalm 121:2)

You may feel you are pretty much abandoned out there. One or two friends may stand beside you. But what can you and your friends do when the enemy is winning? You can grip that sword and continue the fight. And when you are doing the will of the Father, he will provide strength and endurance where there seems to be none. And the victory as well. Celebrate that!

Heavenly Father, some of the readers today need encouragement. They have been fighting their battles pretty much on their own, and for whatever reason they feel like retreating with the others. Lift their sights to see they are not alone—you are standing with them. Make your presence known to them today. Accept their praises for what you are doing. Amen.

When "Grief" Is "Good"

Question: What do the names Lucy and Linus have in common with the expression, "Good Grief"? You know, don't you? Add a third name and the answer will be obvious to you. Charlie Brown.

Peanuts is the name of the comic strip created by the late Charles M. Schultz in 1950. Linus, Lucy, and Charlie have entertained readers since then, along with other characters including Snoopy, Patty, Schroeder, and Pig-Pen. *Peanuts* has appeared in 2,600 newspapers in seventy-five countries. The strip ran without interruption for fifty years. Schultz died on February 12, 2000, and his last original strip ran the next day. What you read today are re-runs.

You remember Linus, don't you? He was the kid who constantly was seen sucking his right thumb, holding a blanket next to his left cheek. But when he was verbal, he was very verbal! In one sequence, Lucy approached Linus, who was seated on the floor. She said, "You and that stupid blanket! Are you gonna carry that thing around the rest of your life? When are you going to learn to stand on your own two feet?" Linus jumped to his feet and declared, rather loudly, "Waddya mean?! I've got just as much will power as anyone else.

See, I don't need this blanket! I can throw it away anytime I want to. Anytime!" He tossed the blanket to the floor, began shaking uncontrollably, whispered "Good Grief," and immediately went to the floor and retrieved the blanket. Lucy said, "You're a hopeless case, Linus…" And Linus replied, "I thought I could do it. I actually thought I could do it" He needed security, and a blanket provided it for him.

We all want to feel secure in our faith, although security is not frequently mentioned in the Bible. It is referred to about twenty times in the Old Testament, and only once in the New Testament. In Hebrews 6, the writer speaks of "hope" as "an anchor for the soul, firm and secure." But we all long for something in which we can find comfort, much like Linus did with his blanket.

The key to feeling secure is finding a time and a place where we can feel safe. Paul Tournier once said, "At the heart of personality is the need to feel a sense of being lovable without having to quality for that acceptance." That acceptance can be found in an invitation given by Jesus, in Matthew 11:28-30.

"Come to me, all of you who are weary and carry heavy burdens, and I will give you rest.

Take my yoke upon you. Let me teach you, because I am humble and gentle, and you will find rest for your souls. For my yoke fits perfectly, and the burden I give you is light."

How inclusive is *that* invitation? Did Jesus really mean "all of you" when he said it? Of course he did. Jesus included everyone in this invitation. And how do people respond? Some shout, "Good grief," like Linus, and they cling to whatever brings them a sense of security and warmth. "It's too good to be true," some might say. "I'm not good enough to be accepted by him," others might argue. Actually, Jesus reached out to everyone when he said, "Come to me, all of you who are weary and carry heavy burdens." He accepts everyone! And the best part is not the acceptance, but the promise he gives: "I will give you rest."

If you know someone whose soul is under siege, share this promise with them. It may be the best news they have heard in a very long time. They can come to Jesus just as they are, even carrying their blanket.

Heavenly Father, I believe your Word is true for all people and all times. My hope is not in the temporal, but the eternal. It is not in the words of teachers and preachers, but in the words of Jesus. I accept his promises as forever promises. My trust is in him. Amen.

Never Lose the Wonder

Few professional athletes achieve greatness after they reach the age of forty. They often reach their physical peak in their twenties and thirties. Exceptions are rare, but there are exceptions.

Matt Bahr definitely was an exception. He was kicking field goals and extra points when he was forty and still playing professional football. If you follow professional football trivia, you may recall that he kicked the winning field goal in Super Bowl XXV, when the New York Giants defeated the Buffalo Bills, 20-19.

On the threshold of his nineteenth year in professional football, Matt Bahr was asked the secret to his longevity. He replied,

"You don't stop playing because you get old; you get old because you stop playing."

You probably know a number of men and women who are in their eighties and are still in the game, so to speak. Evangelist "Gypsy" Smith was once asked how he could continue to be motivated to evangelize at his age. He was 87 at the time. His answer:
"I've never lost the wonder."

Being motivated is not an age thing. It is a wonder thing. You've probably known some young preachers —in their prime years—who lost the wonder and are now doing something else. I've also known some older preachers who didn't need special batteries to keep them going and going but were immensely effective well beyond the time others their age had retired.

How does someone keep the wonder when they have suffered disappointments, hardships, setbacks, loss of loved ones, health problems, and misunderstandings? Here's how.

Here are six suggestions from the Apostle Peter:

1. **Remember who you are.** "You are a chosen people, a royal priesthood, a holy nation, a people belonging to God...." (1 Peter 2:9a NIV)

2. **Remember your mission**. Peter continued, "... that you may declare the praises of him who called you out of darkness into his wonderful light." (1 Peter 2:9b)

3. **Be prepared**. "Therefore, prepare your minds for action." (1 Peter 1:13a) Always maintain your mental preparedness. When asked, let your answer be, "Yes!"

4. **Be ready**. "But just as he who called you is holy, so be holy in all you do." (1 Peter 1:15) Spiritual readiness is not an entitlement. It takes work to maintain a spiritual edge.

5. **Be thankful**. "In this you greatly rejoice, though now for a little while you may have had to suffer grief in all kinds of trials." (1 Peter 1:6)

6. **Be faithful**. "These (trials) have come so that your faith—of greater worth than gold, which perishes even though refined by fire—may be proved genuine and may result in praise, glory and honor when Jesus Christ is revealed." (1 Peter 1:7)

Reflect on these words from singer George Beverly Shea:

**"There's the wonder of sunset at evening,
the wonder as sunrise I see;
But the wonder of wonders that thrills my soul,
is the wonder that God loves me.
There's the wonder of springtime and harvest,
the sky, the stars, the sun;
But the wonder of wonders that thrills my soul,
is a wonder that's only begun."**

Whatever your age—whatever your calling—never lose the wonder.

About the Author
Thomas Elliott Barnard, M.A., Ed.D.

Dr. Tom Barnard is a career college teacher, administrator, minister, and writer. In 2001 he retired as vice-president for institutional advancement at a college in the Boston area. He relocated to Oklahoma City, where he and his wife, Madelyn, currently live.

Tom holds degrees from several public and private universities In 1989 he participated in post-doctoral work at Harvard University's Institute for Educational Management.

For sixteen years Dr. Barnard taught religion and philosophy. His skills as a Bible expositor, story-teller, writer, and public speaker are widely known in educational and religious circles in the States where he has lived.

In 2017 Tom began posting daily prayers on *Facebook*. His commentaries have been well received by readers from all over the Internet world.

Day Break, is his latest book.

Index

Ask and Keep on Asking—6
    Be Happy—It Beats Worry Every Time—8
        Cherish Good Times—Forget the Bad—10
            Defeat Temptation—Look to Jesus—12
                Do One Thing Very Well—14

Face Your Challenges…Courageously—16
    Forgive Me, Please – I Was Wrong—18
        Get Your Spiritual Eyes Checked—20

Give and You Definitively Will Receive—22
    God Hears Prayers—Even Short Ones—24
        God Is with You—Nothing Else Matters—26
           God Keeps His Promises—Always—28
                God Really Cares about You—30

God's Grace Is Just the Thing for You—32
    Halloween Revisited—34

Happiness Is Everything It's Cracked up To Be—36
    Help Is on the Way—Be Encouraged—38
        Hope Is No Small Thing—It's Huge—40
           How Secure Is Your Faith?—42

It's Okay to Draw a Line in the Sand—and Stand—44
    It's Time to Sing Again —46
        Jesus Did It All—48
           Jesus Will Help You Now!—50
                Let God Light Up Your Life—52

Life's Number One Question—54
    Living Upstream in a Downstream World—56
        Look Up, Not Down—58
           Make Winning a Habit—60
                Miracles Still Happen Today—62

Never Lose Hope—God Wins—64
    Out-of-this-World Grace—66
        Perseverance Is Not for Babies—68
            Pursue God—He's Pursuing —70

Push Back Against Negative Thinking—72
    Put Your Pedal to the Metal—74
        Reach out To Jesus—He's Very Close—76

Really Great News—Better than You Think—78
    Relax: God's Timing Is Always Perfect—80
        Right or Wrong—It's Up to You—82
            Seek the Simple Life—84

FRIDAY—Absolutely the Best Day of the Week—86
    Take a Second Look at Eternal Things—88
        Temptation—No Sin in That—90

The Darker the Night—the Brighter the Stars—92
    The Power of the Human Touch—94
        Turn It Over to God—96
            Angels Are Everywhere—98
                Whatever You Do—Do It Well—100

You Are Special—Never Forget That!—102
    You Can Be Number One—104
        You Can't Fly without Wings—106

You Have What You Need—Enjoy It—108
    Never Lose the Wonder—110
        Never Underestimate the Power of Two—112
            When Grief is "Good"—114

The Power of the Human Touch—116
    Give Flowers that Will Never Die—118

What Others Are Saying:

"Dr. Barnard never fails to challenge, to provide fresh insight, and to be so very practical."
Jesse C. Middendorf, D.Min.
Executive Director, Center for Pastoral Leadership, NTS

"I am honored to endorse this new book, *Day Break*. Dr. Barnard's devotionals and meditations are always encouraging and practical."
Gaylene Wallace – ABR, SRS

"Dr. Barnard put his years as a master teacher to work in this fine piece. I find myself rising to a new level when I read his stories and applications."
Doug Eaton –Activator; Businessman

"In his new book, *Day Break*, Dr. Barnard offers meditations that will inspire, inform and encourage the reader. I enthusiastically recommend the book."
W. Talmadge Johnson, M.A., D.D. – G. S. Emeritus, COTN

"I find myself holding my breath in anticipation of each paragraph of Dr. Barnard's devotional writings."
Renda Brumbeloe, M.A.
Retired United Airlines Captain and Writer.

"This book is a banquet of spiritual nourishment."
Kenneth Shelby Armstrong, M.A., Th.D., Ed.D.
Publisher and Writer